PRODUCTIVITY SECRETS FOR STUDENTS

The Ultimate Guide To Improve Your Mental Concentration, Kill Procrastination, Boost Memory And Maximize Productivity In Study

LUCY LOVE

Copyright © 2017

All rights reserved.

ISBN: 9781520357492

TEXT COPYRIGHT © [LUCY LOVE]

all rights reserved. No part of this guide may be reproduced in any form without permission in writing from the publisher except in the case of brief quotations embodied in critical articles or reviews.

Legal & disclaimer

The information contained in this book and its contents is not designed to replace or take the place of any form of medical or professional advice; and is not meant to replace the need for independent medical, financial, legal or other professional advice or services, as may be required. The content and information in this book have been provided for educational and entertainment purposes only.

The content and information contained in this book have been compiled from sources deemed reliable, and it is accurate to the best of the author's knowledge, information, and belief. However, the author cannot guarantee its accuracy and validity and cannot be held liable for any errors and/or omissions. Further, changes are periodically made to this book as and when needed. Where appropriate and/or necessary, you must consult a professional (including but not limited to your doctor, attorney, financial advisor or such other professional advisor) before using any of the suggested remedies, techniques, or information in this book.

Upon using the contents and information contained in this book, you agree to hold harmless the author from and against any damages, costs, and expenses, including any legal fees potentially resulting from the application of any of the information provided by this book. This disclaimer applies to any loss, damages or injury caused by the use and application, whether directly or indirectly, of any advice or information presented, whether for breach of contract, tort, negligence, personal injury, criminal intent, or under any other cause of action.

You agree to accept all risks of using the information presented inside this book.

You agree that by continuing to read this book, where appropriate and/or necessary, you shall consult a professional (including but not limited to your doctor, attorney, or financial advisor or such other advisor as needed) before using any of the suggested remedies, techniques, or information in this book.

TABLE OF CONTENT

Introduction
Understanding Student Attitudes
The 4 Most Popular Types Of Learners
3 Creative Ways Organizing And Managing Your Studying
6 Techniques For Excelling Every Student Should Know
6 Simple Steps To Get Good Marks/Grades In School
The Top 8 Study Habits To Maximize Productivity
The Top 5 Benefits Of Positive Emotions
4 Proven Academic Success Tips
The 80/20 Rule
Conclusion
Check Out Other Books

INTRODUCTION

I want to thank you and congratulate you for downloading the book *"Productivity Secrets For Students: The Ultimate Guide To Improve Your Mental Concentration, Kill Procrastination, Boost Memory And Maximize Productivity In Study"*

A student's life revolves around change and learning. Without learning, our world would simply stop progressing and before you know it, it would perish. Learning constantly, therefore, is a must if one has to progress in life. There are various ways available through which we can learn something new and broaden our horizons in the process. Some of the best ways through which we learn are by reading, listening, observing, watching etc.

In today's time, however, it is not enough to just read and listen, we must go deeper and further than previous generations in our quest for knowledge. In the modern world, the only practical way to do that is get a feel for what it is like to be on the job. The best way to do that is planning and practicing the techniques in this book.

Students need to be well versed when there is the mention of examinations. This is because they show how well students have understood the subject matter. While examinations are very important, it's only a few students who succeed in them. Some of the hindrances to optimum productivity will include:

Regurgitating in-class or lecture material: It's common for students to repeat exactly what was taught in class or what the students read in the library. Although examinations require them to remember what was taught in class, they should not regurgitate the information exactly how it was said by the lecturer. This shows a lack of understanding.

Over-generalization: Many students have fallen into this trap. Inadequate preparation and insufficient details about the specific course or subject details makes students write whatever information that crops up in mind. The overall performance of such student declines drastically.

Carelessness: Many students make careless mistakes that hinder optimum productivity. They fail to adhere to simple instructions and like doing things the way they desire.

Spelling, grammar, and register: Just like carelessness, poor spelling and grammar gives a very negative picture of a student.

If somebody hopes to succeed in their education and learning it is crucial that they can apply a number of education strategies for learners. This book highlights a few exceptionally basic but powerful methods for students to enable them to learn more quickly as well as better their marks greatly.

The picture is quite different today. Getting into any school is not only more expensive but also much tougher. Colleges have become so selective regarding performance since they will consider those who meet their targeted score which is higher.

Because of this, many students are ready to throw their hands in the air and say, "Okay, I get it! I don't have good enough numbers, so I obviously can't go to college. I'll just forget it!" If you are among these, realize this: You, yes YOU, are the reason for this book. It is designed to give you two things: help with what it takes to get into many colleges (and an overview of what happens after you do) and leads on which colleges are eagerly awaiting your application.

Thank you again for purchasing this book, and I hope you enjoy it!

UNDERSTANDING STUDENT ATTITUDES

Many people develop negative thinking and end up having a lot of negativity in their lives. Life has two sides: negative and positive. If you only focus on the negative side, you end up having negative thinking. Once you develop negative thinking and continue seeing things from that negative angle, you will have negative energy. Negative energy in you will develop until it affects your behaviors and attitudes. Having long negative energy will make your attitudes negative towards almost anything. These negative attitudes will negatively influence your personality and you end up being negative. In this situation, you begin to complain about your education, your environment and your life in general. You tend to be unsatisfied about almost anything. Your level of satisfaction and happiness will be minimum.

To reverse this mental/emotional trend, you need to have positive thinking. You need to program your thinking to see things positively. You need to use positive affirmations on a daily basis, in order to help yourself in that direction. Your positivity in your thinking will develop to include positive attitudes & behaviors that will ultimately develop your personality to be positive. Once you begin to see the positive side of life, once you can see things positively, once you condition your thinking towards positivity, only then you can begin to be satisfied with your life. Positive thinking plays a major role in almost anything you see or do. We tend to see things from our own personal angle. We look at things subjectively not objectively. And if we can make that angle positive, we can begin to change. Negative thinking people see the problem rather than the solution. They see the bad side of the situation. If they have an experience which may have two sides, they only recall the dark side of that experience. For example: if they travel to a nice place and have fun for 10 days, but during the last day, they had a mild nuisance or a disturbance, they would only remember that last day, and would label that travel experience as bad. If they go to a nice restaurant and enjoyed the atmosphere, but the waitress was little late for bringing the check, they wouldn't consider coming back to this restaurant. They were programmed to feel and see only the dark side of events.

Attitude is a state of mind, right? Attitude is not something you may touch or see naturally in a person. Attitude is only visible in an individual's manner in a particular situation. If you are a student with a positive attitude then it will help you a lot. A positive attitude has a calming effect on you both physically and mentally. A positive outlook will play a role in giving you the courage to find good opportunities in situations that other individuals lose hope completely. An ideal consideration is avoiding to focus on problems. Instead, allow a positive attitude to guide you in establishing a solution to the problem.

It is a fact that you will be able to achieve the goals you have set for yourself only if you spend your time trying to find a solution for the problems. Keeping a positive attitude is not a very difficult thing. You can easily create a positive thinking system in your mind that focuses on the solution and not on the problems.

You should be happy about what is right in your life instead of crying about all that is wrong in it. You will find that all the successful people in the world have a positive attitude in them. It is not like that they never had any obstacles in their way of success but they dared to fight with those problems with a positive mindset and overcame their problems.

Our brain often forgets the situations we face in our lives but it remembers our mindset and emotions during that situation forever. The emotions are relayed in our actions during problematic situations. For example, when you fail an exam as a student in the early stages of your life, you may forget the reason for failing or worse still you totally forget about the exam. But you may find yourself remembering the feeling of failure you felt at that time for the rest of your life.

This is where the positive attitude comes in play. A positive attitude helps us overcome those feelings. If you keep a negative attitude then your brain will remind you of those feelings of failure, each time even a remote possibility of failure arises in front of you. But a positive attitude always makes you see beyond the situation and help you overcome the feelings of disheartedness and sadness.

The first and the biggest benefit of a positive attitude is that it gives you the strength. When you think with a positive attitude, you receive a sudden optimism about yourself and life. It removes the stress and tension from your lives. It makes your mind avoid the negative and helps you focus on the task in hand.

The main benefit of having a positive attitude is that it helps us achieve our goals. It makes things much easier for us. We also achieve success much faster with a positive attitude than with negative attitude as positive attitude gives us strength to work better and faster. It makes us believe that we can achieve anything in life we aim at.

This belief in life gives us more energy to do things and also keeps us calm and stress-free. Therefore, we stay happy. This is another benefit of having it. A happy mind keeps our body healthy and we are filled with energy and vitality. It also gives us inner strength to fight with the problems. It gives us the power to fight and overcome any difficulty in life. As a student, staying energized will make your learning smooth.

You will notice that if you talk positively and keep a positive attitude in the face of problems, then people will start respecting you more. They will see the strength of your character and will value your company. With the help of inner strength and confidence, you will also get the ability to motivate others to work better.

If I told you there was something that could change your results faster and more dramatically than anything else, would you listen? Would you sign up? Well, pay close attention because the cure is free, readily within your grasp and relatively easy to do - change your attitude, and you change your life.

Williams James said that the greatest discovery of his generation is that you could alter your life by altering your attitude of mind. That said, if there is any aspect of your life that could use a quick positive shift, just fill the prescription Williams offered.

Attitude is among the commonly used, yet most misunderstood, words in the English language - virtually every language in the world has a word for it. Teachers tell their students that if they would just change their attitude they'd get the grades they need. Counselors tell couples that with a better attitude their relationships will improve. Bosses tell their employees to change their attitude if they want to move up (or simply remain) in the company. The medical field encourages patients to keep a good attitude in their efforts to achieve good health.

You'd think that something so critical and that pack's such punch would be a subject that is required in school from the earliest age. Yet, if you asked ten people what attitude means, you'd likely get ten different answers. When you have a clear understanding of just what attitude is and how attitudes are formed, then and only then, you can begin to change it. In truth, only a small percentage of the population controls their attitude. Most of our attitudes are controlled by outside influences; the media, the government, other people, conditions and circumstances in our lives.

So what is attitude? How is it formed? How can we change it to finally get the results we are seeking? Think about cake. Yes, cake. You go to a friend's house and he serves a tasty chocolate cake with peanut butter icing. Do you say, "Wow! Great flour? Great cocoa?" No! You say "Wow! Great cake!" Attitude is kind of like that. Attitude is a mixture, just like the cake - a composite of our thoughts, feelings, and actions.

Further, attitude is not just your thoughts, nor is it just your feelings, but is your thoughts and feelings when combined and expressed in your action. To better understand, consider the relationship of the mind to the body and how the conscious and sub-conscious parts of the mind work together and create the feelings that put us into action that is either positive or negative.

When we work with individuals and organizations, we delve deeply into each part of the mind on its own, and then bring it back together. In this short piece, simply know that you have the choice, the ability, to accept or reject ANY thought that enters your mind from outside sources. STOP! Consider each thought and know that if you choose to accept it, then it is internalized into your sub-conscious mind where it is automatically accepted, automatically turned into emotions and feelings. These feelings, whether they are negative or positive, true or false, are expressed in your actions and perceived by others as your attitude.

You see, it is the body that moves into action as directed by your feelings. If the ideas that are impressed on the sub-conscious mind are confusing, or negative, that will be evident in a person's outward actions. They flit from here to there. They are chaotic, never finishing what they start. Their environment is generally messy and nothing of any consequence is accomplished. Start a project. Abandon it. Start another. Start something else. Disrupt the team. It is said they have a "bad attitude."

Now, when the ideas impressed on the sub-conscious mind are in harmony; when the positive idea is accepted, this too will be expressed in an attitude that is perceived as positive. Such an orderly state shows up as focus. The person is productive and accomplishes more in a short period. They are on task, finish projects on time and begin another. Energize the team. They are seen as having a "good attitude."

Know this. Attitude is a composite of our thoughts, feelings, and actions. In essence, the combination creates a sort of vibration. The thoughts and ideas we choose to get emotionally involved with are expressed in our actions - it shows up as our attitude. Whether these choices are conscious or unconscious matter little. It is still the way it is. You can say you didn't know, but that's too bad, you lose. Don't lose. In life, there is absolutely no allowance for NOT choosing the thoughts and ideas that will serve you well.

When an individual's attitude changes, everything in their life or world shifts, too. If the attitude shifts toward the negative, the person's life shifts in that direction. When the attitude shifts in the positive direction, life improves for the person. Begin now to choose your attitude by choosing your thoughts and ideas. Fill the prescription that James prescribed, and take daily!

THE 4 MOST POPULAR TYPES OF LEARNERS

There are different types of learners that use different methods to learn. Finding out which learner a student is and how they learn is an important task to achieve. With society changing rapidly, the need for a solid education and excellent communication skills are important. Students might have wondered how a person in their class can never take notes or wondered why a person took so many notes or maybe even wondered why they had the person in their class who asked too many questions. Understanding learning patterns will help a great deal.

There are visual learners who intake information by listening. Auditory learners take information by seeing. Kinesthetic learning, who intake information by actually using; and last but not least read and write learners, who, well intake information by reading and writing. Multisensory learning is known to be very helpful for students who have learning disabilities. These students often have trouble learning in basic subjects such as writing, reading, math and expressive language. With this technique, students are in a position to use more of their own personal strengths to help engage them in the learning development and the benefits are definitely rewarding. Not sure what type of learner you are? Well, there are several different signs to look for when determining what kind of learner you are.

1st Type:

The first learning type is the "Visual Learner!" This learner is the one that no matter how much they are taught, they can never really grasp the information unless they write it down. Visual learners prefer to read to gain a full understanding. Visual learners are excellent at spelling. In most of the cases, they were in all of the ***spelling bee competitions*** while kids. They are also the ones who can never remember names. Quiet time is also important to this type since they have to process what is being said. Writing essays or stories tend to come easy for this type of person, as well as, taking notes.

To determine if a student is a visual learner, there are a few things to look for. Visual learners seem to recall information the best by actually seeing it. They majorly pay attention to detail and are likely to be organized, like to read and would rather watch someone teach them something, rather than actually learning hands on or talking about it. You may also notice that these types of learners may have a hard time following directions, verbally and tend to be distracted by sound/noise.

2nd Type:

The second learning type is the "Auditory Learner!" This type of learner is the one who will learn by simply listening to what is being said/explained/taught to them. Focusing on words and understanding their meanings are more effective than writing it down. You can normally spot this type of learner because they love to talk. This type is the person that you hear talking aloud and not afraid to speak in class or any situation. They are also very good at explaining something that was communicated to them through the spoken word. Some of the things that this person can learn from are to watch videos, taping the notes from class and then going back to write them down, repeating the words over and over to themselves. So, to ask this person to stop talking for a long period of time in a class setting could be quite a task for a teacher or professor.

Auditory or aural learners learn best by listening to the information being explained/taught to them. These types of learners tend to ask for instructions and retain information through verbal communication like open discussions and lectures. They are not big fans of graphs, charts or puzzles as they often feel confused when items like these are presented to them. They are very good at note taking.

3rd Type:

The third learning type is the "Kinesthetic Learner!" This learner learns by doing. You will find that when it comes to education such students might have a tough time since most classes don't require physical activity. With this information, I wonder if teachers recognize that it's hard for this type of learner to sit and be quiet. This learner is the one, who can study with the music turned up loud, takes several study breaks, enjoys role-playing and thrive on memory type games. Textbooks and reading tend to be boring for them and they can struggle with note taking.

A Kinesthetic or tactile learner performs best with more practical methods. These students may seem engaged while in the science lab, like to build things, and tend to be good at sports. You will also notice that they may not be great at spelling, probably get bored very quickly with lectures and discussions and may not be very good at spelling and don't perform well with long tests and writing essays.

Concrete learners have their focus on audio-visuals, games and pair work. Analytical learners center their preference on self-correction, verbal-linguistic activities, and structured study methods and texts.

There is the category of communicative learners who are good in role playing, realia, and simulations. Authority-oriented learners take copious notes, use of manipulatives and are eager for detailed explanations.

4th Type:

Finally, the fourth learning type is read and write learner. This type absolutely loves writing and enjoys reading textbooks. You will find that they learn better when information is written, such as keywords, rather than watching or listening. They do well learning alone by writing out items in their own words to absorb information that was taught to them. You may also find these types of learners digging into dictionaries, glossaries and handouts.

3 CREATIVE WAYS ORGANIZING AND MANAGING YOUR STUDYING

Organized Time Management

When in the course of your life it becomes evident that you can't simply do everything you want to do in good time, you need to do a bit of thinking. This is also true if you are, for example, in college. College time management is, therefore, a must. When in college, you are wearing a number of proverbial hats: you have classes to go to, papers to write, and just go on with everyday living. Given all this, it behooves you to come to terms with the necessity of managing your time.

Everyone is a captive of time. No matter what path you are treading, and as a student, you always check the nearest timepieces to prevent yourself from being late or to catch up on things that have to be done. For others, injecting a little time to relax and have fun during a busy day could be difficult, but for some, juggling studies, relaxation, and time for themselves is as easy as breathing. Why? This is because the latter has mastered time management. If you belong to the former type of individuals, then maybe you should work on these useful time management tips:

Goal setting is the first and the most important factor for successful time management. When you set a goal, you are aware of what you want and accordingly keep time aside. However, you should ensure that you set realistic goals that are not too tough or demanding. Also, be specific in what you want to achieve. This will help remove the risk of vagueness for your goals.

Have a to-do list. The first step that you should do in order to organize your schedule at least for the whole week is to write the things that need to be accomplished in the next seven days. Effective time management should be planned and accomplished on a daily but not on an hourly basis.

Prepare your next-day schedule. Time management does not only involve making a schedule for the entire week. In your everyday activity, preparing a list of things you need to do the next day before the day ends is important. This list will help you be reminded of the errands or activities you need to be done the following day.

Do two or more things at the same time. Time management is about using your time productively. To manage and save time effectively, you should learn to do some other things simultaneously.

Follow your schedule and keep logs. To ensure that you would accomplish everything listed on your schedule, follow it religiously so your time management exercises can work effectively. Note your activities and the time taken to complete it. This will allow you to gauge the places where you are wasting time. Minimize wastage and increase the value of every second spent. Preparing logs may seem time-consuming, but ultimately you are the one who is going to benefit the most.

Learn to prioritize. It is vital for you to pinpoint which among your scheduled tasks should be prioritized. Focus your attention on what's on top of the list and accomplish them. Try to do as many things as you can for the day. For example, based on your priority and convenience, you can either spend the bulk of your time in books or by going through online study materials. Your goals should be a guiding factor in prioritizing things.

Time management strategies can extend far beyond efficiency. Using time wisely is essential even in times of crises. In the most serious of situations, time management can literally be a lifesaver. You might face a profound challenge at any moment, so now is the perfect time to develop strong crisis management and time management skills!

Organizing Your Space

You have an exam next week. You are there, you can't concentrate on studying. You get lost in thoughts or you start dozing off. The answer to this predicament is being able to manage your study space. You will require a specific region in your room or at home. The area should have the appropriate furnishings, a personal touch, and some planning. Such a setting will help boost your results.

First, you need to personalize the space. Place decorations that will motivate you when you are almost giving up. With the knowledge of your personality, you may go for negative or positive motivators. It may be the previous essay you performed poorly or that luxurious destination you dream traveling to after passing your final examination. Match the space with the colors you adore.

You will need to Organize your study materials in different binders depending on the subject or course. Ensure they are marked for easy retrieval. You may also go ahead to organize your computer files and apply descriptive names to them.

Ensure that you are comfortable. But do not be too comfortable to save yourself from falling asleep. The bed should be avoided by all means. Your study room should be in a way that the desk and chair allow good posture. Sit facing away from the window to avoid distractions.

Clean up the study space to eliminate distractions like excess clutter. Place your phone aside or switch to airplane mode in case you using it as a study tool like a calculator. Place some background music that suits you.

Keep things at hand. Your studying materials and supplies should be closer. This will ensure that you don't get up from your desk too often.

If you live on campus, your dorm room may be too loud if your roommate has a lot of friends passing through regularly. If this is the case, you may be better off trying to study in a notably quieter place such as the library. It is best to locate an area that is serene, with little to no traffic of any kind and without auditory, sensory or visual distractions (i.e. no loud music, no wind, and no people). If it is hard to locate a sacred spot for studying, invest in a pair of noise-cancelling headphones. You can purchase a good pair for about fifty bucks ... your return on investment will be invaluable.

Organize Yourself

Have you gotten yourself in that awkward moment you are in front of your door only to realize that you forgot to carry your key? Now, do you remember a moment having convinced yourself that you had all your books packed for class and once in class, the truth dawns on you? You don't have the books with you! This is why organizing yourself is so important.

Do you normally rush? Do you find it easy? The reality is you should not rush. Point blank. Always wake up early enough for school. You will be in a position to arrive at school early enough ahead of time. If it takes you 30 minutes to wake up, take a shower and dress up, cover that time by ensuring that you wake up 45 minutes earlier before your departure. Place your clock in the far corner of the room to ensure that you are not tempted to switch the alarm off and going back to sleep.

You need to refresh your wardrobe, right? Make it a habit for each night before going to bed. Carefully chooses, iron and lay out your clothes that you will have to use the next day. This makes you set for the morning since your clothes will be ready.

Cluttering!! Ooh Noo!! Avoid clutter by all means. When the school year begins, you do not have clutter around you. Be careful not to build any as the year builds up. Make folders file school announcements, any graded tests, papers to be given to parents or whatever the tasks you have at hand. Do away with outdated papers such as for the events that have already passed.

Timing! What is the secret? Your study time should be broken up. Use a good planner to ensure that you have enough study hours. For instance, if you may require seven hours to study for an exam, you can break the hours into six equal one-hour sessions. Be consistent in your study times and avoid cases of studying and cramming the last minute.

Broccoli and dessert! Are you curious to know what am aiming at? Make sure that you eat the broccoli first before dessert. When you are studying or taking your homework, tackle the hard subjects first before moving to the easier ones. You will have a breeze and enjoy what you are doing.

Make it a habit to get help where you haven't understood. Get assistance from your teacher, friend, sibling or parent. Whoops! Do not give up when things go berserk.

Do you ever reward yourself? When you achieve your set goals, how do you reciprocate yourself for the effort? Reward yourself. For example, a night out at the movies or a tour to the park. You will always be motivated.

When studying for exams, it may feel (at times) that you live in a prison. To ensure success with your studies, it is imperative to take some time for yourself. Though it may seem counter-intuitive, this is one of the most critical and effective study habits to adopt. Provided you don't pollute your brain with the distractions, it is a good practice to take approximately 15 minutes to relax and quiet your mind. This allows your brain to absorb and catalog the information it has just received. Of course, the time needed varies among individuals so experiment to see what works best for you.

These breaks will help you to retain what you have studied instead of mentally "running out of the room". Imagine that your brain is like a flower in a flower pot. Every bit of information that you study is like water. If you put in too much water too fast, you will drown the flower; however, if you pour a little water in, let the flower and soil absorb the water and repeat the process, then the flower grows up and flourishes. Treat your study sessions like you are watering a flower.

6 TECHNIQUES FOR EXCELLING EVERY STUDENT SHOULD KNOW

Is Academic success important? I went around trying to establish what most students stand for when it comes to academic success. Wait! The majority of students have a busy schedule to balance between jobs and classes. It pushes them to have the zeal to succeed amid financial challenges and other distractions. The question that hits your mind now is, 'What are the right techniques for excelling?'

Technique 1: Be Curious And Adventurous Academically

Curiosity is basic human instinct. Curiosity is explained as a strong desire to know about something. A curious tendency of self-instills a relentless desire for knowing something hidden or concealed. Conceptually, a systematic curious attitude towards knowledge enhancement shapes students. Literally, the student should be an individual who is studying at a school, college, university, etc. Studying is an activity of learning or gaining knowledge. An educator satisfies inquisitiveness of students. A student is knowledge-seeker, while an educator is knowledge-giver. A purposefully designed interactive setup of knowledge-seekers and knowledge-givers shapes educational institutions. It is noteworthy that a learning environment is designed to shape excellent students. An excellent student is the ultimate goal of multiple knowledge management activities, both academic and non-academic. An excellent student is curious basically, but creative ultimately. A curious student wants to know something unknown, now and then, while, a creative student wants to make something anew, now and again. When a student is curious, they have the zeal to unearth ultimate truths as they develop a bond with what they learnt in the past. They, therefore, have a foundation of excelling since everything is understood from revision.

Technique 2: Pick Classes Strategically

Some classes are crucial towards attaining your degree while a large percentage are electives. There is always room for students to choose the required classes. Ensure you choose classes and professors that are compatible with your personality and favorites. This is a recipe for good grades.

Technique 3: Be Active During Class Lessons

Students enhance their knowledge level through absorbing lectures/syllabus. Learning through lecture is the easiest way of gaining knowledge. An excellent student reads the learning matter before the lecture, pays full attention on subject matter during the presentation, participates in learning activity through relevant/thought-provoking questions, she/he makes notes of important points during knowledge transfer, after the lecture, she/he reviews noted points and prepares personal notes. A learning approach based on Preparation, Attention, Participation, Notes-Construction and Revision is an effective learning strategy.

Technique 4: Join A Study Group

Find strength in a Study Group. Some challenging classes will require you to consult and a study group comes out as essential. Students will come together to share their research and brainstorm. You get to understand the concept you didn't master.

Technique 5: Sleep Well

What about sound sleep!! Many are the times when you will find many students sacrificing their sleep as they attempt to juggle a social life, jobs, and classes. It is a practice detrimental to your academic career and health as well. Being sleep deprived exerts pressure on your mind making it not to perform at full capacity. Sleep well to ensure that your mind is fresh to grasp most of what is taught during class lessons.

Technique 6: Take breaks between studies and avoid cramming

Make consistent study habits and avoid cramming. You will end up overdoing it on a particular subject and the expense of the rest. Efficiency is attained when there is adequate or even spacing in your reading and studying.

Is multitasking right? Most of you will say yes to this question. The truth is set some time aside special for studying and avoid distractions like in-person conversations with pals, being on internet or phone calls. Keep them at the minimum and focus your mind on studying at that particular time. Take around five minute breaks for every 25 minutes.

6 SIMPLE STEPS TO GET GOOD MARKS/GRADES IN SCHOOL

Education is a student's key to achieving dreams and aspirations in life. It is also the key to achieving the career path you want to have in the future. However, the road would not be easy because in order for a student to achieve their dreams they need to study first and get good or high grades in their school.

Being in high school is fun and also difficult for most parts. There are also a lot of distractions and pressure. The toughest part though is the pressure to get higher grades in order to get to college and eventually graduate and pursue a career. Staying in school can be very hard but with hard work and inspiration you can finish with flying colors.

There isn't any magic formula to the reality that to achieve good marks you must study, even so learning how to secure great grades by means of studying isn't something that every student comes by effortlessly. Once people are going to college they require all the assistance they can get not only with having good marks, but the study methods that get them to this place.

Step 1: Commit Yourself to School

Any time you genuinely desire to get A's and B's all of it starts with making classes a top goal in your daily life. If you decide to go meet up with your friends instead of staying home and study, you'll discover it is difficult to get good grades with that impending exam. The majority of college students that want to understand tips to get good marks recognize that they must dedicate a good portion of their time to studying.

Set a percentage of time to study daily, ensure your studying is done before you begin undertaking anything else. If you're having a problem in a particular topic or have an important examination coming up, you may want to boost your study time. The more familiar you are with the subject matter in a specific class the higher your chances will be to receive a better grade.

Step 2: It's Every bit as Essential that You Get Prepared

You wouldn't be the first student to forget your books in class or neglect to turn an assignment in, nevertheless, no college student could do this for very long yet still retain an excellent mark. Make a practice of making certain when you attend school each day you take everything that you need for the entire day.

Prior to deciding to sit down to study ensure you have all the things you will need for your studying, such as paper, instruments for writing, notes, as well as textbooks. The better structured you are the more successful your studying will likely be. Last of all be sure you have a relaxing area to study where there won't be any interruptions.

Step 3: Revise

Passing exam is about practice and expressing the system. Practice does create perfectly. Exercise past papers, sit down for the time allocated, do the examination under exam condition, get your paper marked and get a superior response.

A few students are just good at the exam. This can be a priceless plus in school, and university. But their IQ isn't inevitably particularly high. Their classmates might be much cleverer and might grasp things faster in lecture and put in the equal effort when it comes to revision. The secret is quite easy and most students think that they know about it already. The trick is PAST EXAM PAPERS. They are the syllabus, they are the workbook, they are everyone you require to be successful and get great examination results. Past examination papers are NOT just for testing your awareness - they're for obtaining it. Just earlier than you drift off to sleep, make a picture of yourself effectively carrying out your examination.

What I usually do is to learn the notes - this can be done simply by highlighting the key words and then remembering them. By doing so, you can string the sentence in concert very well. This is what I usually do - if I have enough time:-

1. Read from end to end the notes in brief

2. Show up the keywords (not just a few, but ALL)

3. Learn the keywords and try to string them into a sentence; make sure you can speak out each of the keywords because most of the times, marks are awarded when the keywords are present.

4. Do again step 3 several times

5. Get anyone to examination you and see if you can remember what's in the notes

6. Do many of practice assignments - as a lot of as you can, so you know how to apply what you have memorized?

7. Read through the notes some more times

8. Have a superior night's sleep and be ready

Must you have a need of time and are in dire straits:-

1. Show up everyone the keywords and memorize

2. Repeat step 1 two times

3. Do several practice assignments?

Step 4: Don't Be Reluctant to Set Objectives

Occasionally if you discover it difficult to stay self-disciplined, goal setting is just the thing you need to remain focused. Think about what you want to undertake, it might be to have all A's in your classes or it could be to gain access to the university you have your heart set on. There's nothing more inspiring than an objective to work for in relation to encouraging you to study each day.

Step 5: Learn to Study

Not everyone knows how to get exceptional scores effortlessly, a lot of us, have to be taught productive study behaviors. This can consist of making up a study plan, taking excellent notes, and making use of many of the resources at your disposal to make sure you comprehend the materials well. Learning to study is only one component of getting excellent grades, however, for many students, the lack of these details may show in their scores.

Step 6: Take care of Yourself

An important part of learning to get excellent marks is to take proper care yourself. You cannot study efficiently or do well on your examinations if you can't receive ample rest as well as eat correctly. Your mind requires rest and energy to accomplish its best. Getting good grades is one thing anybody can accomplish, it's a question of learning, as well as the drive and self-control to do so.

You'll get more chances of topping your exams when you review your notes every single night when you get home than when you don't. Our teacher used to give us tests every day and it helped us, students, a lot to familiarize every subject since we were forced to study every night in preparation for the following day's test.

If you combine determination with your good study habits, there is no way for you not to get that first honor award you have been struggling to achieve for a long time now. Be persistent in your daily studies and dare not to give up. Most of all, enjoy school.

THE TOP 8 STUDY HABITS TO MAXIMIZE PRODUCTIVITY

Habit 1: Be Self-Motivated

Self-motivation is a key towards goal attainment. Be driven by willpower and optimism. Motivating one's self varies according to your purpose in life. Students are always doing their best in order to finish their degree and find a better job in the future. Those students who fail to endure and keep a positive attitude will never make it until the end. We have different priorities in life as well as objectives and goals. You can never accomplish what you are aiming for if you don't have enough confidence to make it happen. Helping your own self is the most important thing in life. How can you help your fellow students and build your dreams if you don't have the guts to do it?

Build self-esteem by reading books about the philosophies of education. A student who is full of potentials and abilities has a high level of confidence. Understand yourself very well. Learn to identify your limitations and abilities so that you will be able to gauge your own capacities and weaknesses.

Habit 2: Plan the first week and see how things go

Make any required adjustments for the following week, and continue adjusting until you have devised a strategy that works. Include 15 minutes before the end of each day to review the next day's routine. You are going to be surprised at how helpful this step can be. Doing this before the end of the day will arrive in handy in case you overlooked something you need for tomorrow that should be taken care of within that day. At the really least you'll minimize surprises, even save yourself some grief, and at greatest, you will be totally prepared for tomorrow's classes. A word of caution: don't routine your days so tightly which you have no flexibility to deal using the unexpected. Leave a little wiggle room to accommodate those unanticipated situations that inevitably crop up.

Habit 3: Analyze the material prior to you go to course

This might not have been necessary in high school. But with the quantity and depth of substance covered in every class at the university level, you'll be behind before class even starts should you not take the time to become acquainted using the substance prior to you stepping into the classroom. You'll be relieved, if not pleasantly surprised, at how much simpler you will absorb the lecture after you've made the effort to familiarize yourself with the subject beforehand.

Habit 4: Analyze every day

Studies show that students who create time to study on a daily basis are better placed than students with much more sporadic study habits, and much better than those who cram. How much time do you ought to study? A rule of thumb for effective study abilities is to devote three several hours a week for research and learning for every credit hour. If your biology class is three credit several hours, then you ought to invest approximately 15 several hours a week on homework and learning outside the classroom. If you're taking a total of 15 credit several hours, then you ought to be spending upwards of 45 hours per week on homework and learning. When you think about it, committing to an everyday analyze schedule is really the only choice you have for obtaining in all the hours needed for learning and homework each week.

Habit 5: Stay Focused And Say NO To Distractions

The feeling is widely known by most college students.... that moment there is a lot of work to be done yet you have minimal time available to you. The focus matters in such a situation. In college, it is overwhelming when you have to deal with staying in shape, balancing your relationships, and having excellent grades. Distractions are all over but you need to keep the focus on what is important for you.

You need some time alone. Always treasure some 10 to 15 minutes to soul search. Take this time to clear the mind, be aware of your feelings and think what matters on that day. Just walk around or focus on meditation.

Do you own the week? Are you a property that the week owns? Life is unpredictable and fun as a student. Schoolwork is important and you need to set time to complete. Write down activities for the week and ensure you are timely in undertaking them.

Maintain a diary or a notebook to be writing down the lists. When done, mark it out from the list. Avoid your phone by switching it off during study hours. It is hard to focus on your studies while your phone is ringing, when emails are popping up, or your friends are insisting you go out.

To stay focused, learn to say 'NO'. It comes in handy when you have placed a lot of value on yourself and your studies.

Habit 6: Do Not Procrastinate

Learn the art of discipline. Most students unconsciously procrastinate when they get distracted from what they are supposed to do. Learning self-discipline will help a student resist distractions and focus on the task at hand.

Think of a reason to start working on your task. Taking the first step to complete a task is a start to beat procrastination. Most students usually find their groove when exam time is at the corner.

Stick to the day's plan. Plans are made to ensure that a student accomplishes the tasks needed for the day. If something comes up, take note but stick to the plan.

Prioritize With the FI-FO Method. One of the most important Effective Study Habits is how you prioritize your classwork. Often when you are stuck on a hard test question the advice is to skip ahead and go back to it later, but this strategy can backfire when it comes to studying. The term FI-FO means First-In First-Out and it helps to keep you focused on the task at hand. By remembering FI-FO you will implement a system that keeps you organized and less overwhelmed.

Habit 7: Start Working Smart

Working SMART is cliché to most of you, right? It does not matter the number of times you have heard of it, but what matters is implementing the technique. Working smart in your education ensures that you excel and be on top of the rest. An excellent student sets goals with SMART properties.

Schooling is a difficult process and one where everybody has a different outcome at the end. Many of us look back and think that we could have put that little bit more effort in, and while it's unfair to be too critical there are some simple ways to becoming a successful student.

Do you desire to be a student who is successful? Get the secrets on how to hold this title. On a yearly basis, this seems to be something that is becoming clearer to all and sundry. Everyone is different; their makeup and mindsets are never the same. But, there are a few staples to think about when looking for the key ingredients of successful students. These are:

- **Participation** - The best way for us to learn is to experience it, and with this in mind, classroom participation is an integral part of this. Activity participation is exactly what is needed to be involved in - ask questions, offer solutions and be honest when they don't understand something. As the cliché goes: "someone who asks a question is stupid for five minutes, someone who doesn't ask is stupid forever." This is, of course, difficult for students due to the peer pressure but participation is integral to growth.

- **Attention** - It's a fact that people need to be attentive to learn what they are doing or to do a good job. They should always be looking to improve learning and be aware of exactly what it is that is happening around them. Don't read or talk when you're supposed to be listening.

- **Active** - Students shouldn't let time go to waste, the twiddling of thumbs is never a viable option. Always do work outside the classroom and complete homework properly. Always be active when you are in lessons.

- **Effort** - Always remember that the grades aren't what determines a successful or unsuccessful student; it's about getting out what you put in. Some students don't need to be studying as hard as others, but if you put in the effort to reach your goals then that means that you are a success. While some think that grades are the begin all and end all of life, the truth is that if the end of school gets you to where you want to be then that means a student is a success.

- **Enthusiasm** - This is a tough thing to achieve but mixing a desire to learn with lessons that spark debate is the best way of finding students that are successful. People always need the desire to improve.

Habit 8: Reduce Stress (in study)

If all else does not work out, do not press the panic button. Stress can make it much harder for you to definitely understand as well as recall things out of your studying sessions. If you find yourself having a panic attack, try taking some deep breathing plus slow your brain down by simply thinking about something happy. It is best to actually practice it prior to the exam day. Finally, never converse with other people right after the tests about how it went, it might have an effect on some other exams within the day.

Exam stress is easier to deal with when you have prepared correctly and taken control of your study sessions. Organizing your study sessions in the months leading up your exams requires that you prepare a study schedule and stick with it. The study schedule should have school, social, travel, sport and even downtime on it. The schedule should be at least a month in advance so you work around the unexpected events. The final thing about your study schedule it should always be with you, either on your phone or written down in a diary.

Eat the right foods and exercise, will help you reduce your exam stress and allow you to maximize your performance during the final exams. With the correct nutrition, you can actual increase your intelligence during the exams. Foods like Honey are actual shown to increase intelligence and also help with stress. Where the opposite can be seen when you have too much-refined sugar. The right food only helps to a point, you also need exercise. It would be a good idea to get into the habit of 30 minutes early each morning and also during the exams. Workouts reduce your stress during the lead up to the exams and then on the exams. The second benefit is when you exercise regularly you improve memory and learning.

Avoid fellow students who distract you. One way to reduce stress is to simply stay away from stressful students. If you have a study partner that is complaining about how much studying they have to do and who is really worried about the upcoming test, you may want to study by yourself instead. You may also want to avoid students who take up too much of your time. Your friends may want to go out with you and have a good time but if you are preparing for an important test, you have to be willing to pass on the occasional night out.

THE TOP 5 BENEFITS OF POSITIVE EMOTIONS

Are you ready to increase your positivity ratio? Let this be your everyday drive. Increasing positive emotions will require you to identify and track your emotions. Give much focus on the specific emotion and struggle to improve it. Do you know about positivity treasure chest? You ought to embrace it so that you are rejuvenated daily.

Benefit 1: Creativity and Productivity!

Take a minute and question yourself when you feel more creative and productive. Is it when you are happy or angry? Is it when you feel hopeful or dejected? What negative emotions do is to push you towards knee-jerk, positive emotions open up your field of vision. You will be motivated towards attending your lessons, carrying out brilliant researches and your creativity will increase. Ultimately, this generates into a very productive student.

Benefit 2: Less Stress

Positive emotions foster efficient, balanced and synchronized physiological patterns in the nervous and cardiovascular systems. In good health state, you are able to avoid responses induced by negative stress and your revision is made easy. You will give maximum concentration during class lessons and thus grasp a lot of content without straining.

Benefit 3: Helping Other Students

Have you ever felt the beauty of helping others in your class? Understand the dynamics of positive emotions for you to be in a position to help others achieve their goals and dreams. Give them a smile, a wonderful handshake, a joyous greeting, a spirit-uplifting comment or a pat on the back. This will brighten the day of your friends. Positive emotions create a positive atmosphere to improve the progress of everyone and empower them.

Benefit 4: Increases Attention Capacities

Positive emotions increase a student's attention, memory, and awareness.

Students will, therefore, take in more information, understand how ideas relate to each other and ability to hold several ideas in the brain at an instance.

Benefit 5: Exploration

Positive emotions help students to open up to new possibilities. Learning and building on skills increases making it easier to perform tests or tasks.

4 PROVEN ACADEMIC SUCCESS TIPS

Tip 1: How to Remember Anything

Get Enough Sleep - Sleep Improves Memory

ZZZZZZZZZZZZZZZZzzzzzzzzzzzzzzz ... Oh, we must have dozed off - so much for effective study habits. Just kidding ... however, it is a great practice to make sure you sleep 6 to 8 hours each night. This is essential before taking any test or exam. Adequate sleep allows your mind to fully relax and begin focusing on the task at hand. The age-old practice of "pulling all-nighters" and "cramming" for exams is actually counter-productive. You see, when you are sleep deprived, your body produces stress hormones that can impair brain function. So, students who get adequate sleep tend to have better grades.

If you have observed how overly-stressed people seem to overlook things a lot and become increasingly more unproductive the longer they stay stressed, this is because their minds are no longer operating properly due to the stress. It is vital that one allows his mind and body rest regularly. Aside from obtaining the full eight hours of sleep each night, students are even more efficient and productive at class if they could get rest for about 10 to 15 minutes in the afternoon, also. Sleep and rest enable the brain cells to recoup from all the data and also activities it has obtained and done the whole day. Because of this, your own brain's ability to maintain the condition of its memory space keeps intact and in good shape. Learning ability increases when you nurture your brain with a good sleep and other healthy habits.

Eat Right - Foods that Boost Memory

You ought to always get a balanced diet to negate the impact of memory loss. Always plan at least five to seven servings of vegetables and fruits in your daily diet. This helps to ward off the effect of free radicals on the brain cells. However, it is easier said than done. It is nearly impossible to find wholesome food these days and work pressure forces you to rely heavily on processed food. Under such circumstances, it is vital that you take to using high-quality natural and organic supplements to ensure that your body gets a daily supply of antioxidants.

Along with the activities and also rest you give for your brain, it's also vital that you nurture your mind with essential goodness. Omega-3 fatty acids, in particular, are extremely beneficial to the mind, because it improves the health of the mind and improves memory capacity. Eat foods loaded with this specific nutrient, such as fish, garlic, and essential olive oil. Along with Omega-3, a person should also consume a lot of fruits and veggies to get anti-oxidants within the body. Eating lean meat and poultry without the skin also add to the health and capacity of the brain. Avocado, blueberries, rosemary, coconut oil, beans and legumes, nuts, spinach, and broccoli are good at improving your memory and concentration naturally.

Get A Healthy Dose Of Exercise - Physical Exercises Help Boost Memory

A healthy body leads to a healthy mind. We're all informed of the bodily benefits of exercise, but regular exercise can also help the mind's ability to think, store and also remember details. Make it a habit of exercising every day. It is one of the sure-fire methods to negate memory loss. It is more helpful if the exercise that you involve in is aerobic in nature. According to studies, people who engaged in moderate walking exercises a few times in a week outperformed couch potatoes after about six months. Work-outs reduces stress levels, improves blood flow to the brain, and enables you to sleep well. When blood flow is increased, more nutrients and oxygen arrive at their target parts. Therefore, as the body becomes fit, your head becomes healthy too. All these contribute to preventing memory loss.

Physical exercises make the brain be sharp. Good health and vitality help to maintain a strong memory that is essential when executing simple mathematical problems, puzzles, writing essays or studying for exams.

Tip 2: Speed Reading for Success: Read to Absorb More Information than Ever Before!

This technique is related to empowering the brain or channeling it for speed-reading. There are some simple techniques that can help you achieve success. This method helps in improving reading speed as well as comprehension. It will enable you to activate the brain's memory and visual span enlargement technique. Here are some details about those methods.

Step 1 - Structure: This technique of speed-reading focuses on the structure of the book. Every section of a book has an introduction, body and conclusion. To improve your reading speed, simply read the first introductory paragraph and the conclusion. It will help you to understand the meaning. Skimming through the body will give you more hints.

Step 2 - Chunking: This is an important part of speed reading. Chunking means grouping multiple words and reading them together. It is more of a visual reading. With this technique, the brain is able to process the text faster. This interrelated and interdependent grouping of words is a novel way of reading.

Step 3 - Hand Motion: Following words with a finger is another excellent way of fast reading. It improves focus and concentration.

Step 4 - Word Skipping: Skipping common words while reading is another method of improving speed. Common words could be "I", "the", "an" etc. Learn to skip one word at a time. For instance, if you have learned to skip the word "the", then take up a new word and practice skipping it. It will definitely improve speed reading.

Step 5 - Vocabulary: You can increase your reading speed when you master a better and improved vocabulary. When you know the meaning of the words that you read, it is easy to comprehend. You will not waste time by thinking about word meaning.

Step 6 - Scanning and Review: Scanning helps in preparing the brain to comprehend text. When you read through the titles, subtitles, bulleted text etc, you get an idea of what's in it for you. Spending a few seconds on pictures, captions and keywords help a great deal in improving online speed reading.

Step 7 - Sub-Vocalization: It means the inner voice. If you read quietly, the words are not spoken aloud. This silent reading is slower as compared to loud reading. If you want to improve speed reading, read the text aloud. It is not easy to break the habit of silent reading, but you can begin with one page a day and gradually get into the habit of reading aloud.

Improving vocabulary is also one of the most important ways of increasing your reading speed. In addition to this, it also improves your verbal communication.

Tip 3: Study Less by Studying More Efficiently

As a student, you will need better grades and less stress during your academic period. You will find it fit to have fewer hours studying and more free time to yourself. Decide to use things like visualizing and metaphors. Do not be too much of a perfectionist, just work on ideal dreams of achieving your certification.

Apply the use of case studies. It will aid you in understanding how real people improve grades by having to study and stress less. Negotiate a three-month action plan that is realistic and concrete. Do not procrastinate.

Take good notes in the soonest time possible. Note down any cues to the notes and questions along the left column. Give brief summary at the end of each section. Cues are important too when studying the notes at a later moment and summaries help in synthesizing of information and prioritization of certain areas. Always reflect on the notes and question yourself why the topic or section is important and how they connect to what you already know.

Tip 4: Wonderful Studying Techniques

Technique 1: SQ3R technique

Survey, Question, Read, Recite, and Review or popularly known as SQ3R technique is very effective for you to manage your studying time as well as your skills. By asking yourself questions that are based on what you have studied from your book or notes is very effective study system that works for many students.

Technique 2: Break Between Studies For Brain Relaxation

When you are studying, it would be beneficial if you take 10 to 15 minutes break. This is important because it helps your brain to rest for a while and collect information on very successfully.

Technique 3: Use of Mind Maps

Mind maps offer an outstanding way to study for exams which will include a substantial amount of relevant information. Mind maps let you display relations between ideas, which makes it simple for you to not forget the information covered. For that matter, by simply designing your very own mind maps and utilizing those to study, simply beginning with several pertinent terminologies will help you to remember most of the course with no problem.

Technique 4: Memorization

Condensing together with memorization materials are another great study option to utilize when you are thinking about, how would you study for exams? To make use of this kind of study technique, you begin by writing out all you need to know for the exam. Next, take the primary pages and make an effort to condense all of them without taking away content material - merely concentrate on eliminating terminology which is pointless. And then continue repeating this method right up until you've got everything condensed to a page or two.

Technique 5: Use of Flashcards

Of all the numerous strategies to study for exams, flashcards are one of the oldest, most favored methods. This study approach is very effective in the event that you are getting ready for a test in a course that requires you to definitely remember a number of terms. Flashcards can be used for term memorization, to master images or perhaps to write down theories. Produce your very own flashcards and study them frequently.

Technique 6: Study Practices

Now while you still wondering how do you study for examinations? It's helpful to produce some great study practices that conform to your own study methods of choice. These are critical study practices that you need, to get your finest scores.

Keep away from cramming, never be in the situation of analyzing half the night prior to an examination. Waiting around to begin studying the night prior to the examinations would mean that you aren't learning the material effectively and also on the day of your exam you won't find a way to remember the info. It's very easy to avoid cramming simply put together your review periods in the lead up to the actual exams. Splitting your own study periods into 30 times will make them far better to understand material for the tests

THE 80/20 RULE

The 80/20 principle is where you focus on the top most productive 20% of things to achieve 80% of your results. The principle is very important to students when they are unsettled about their education and other aspects of their life. Placing the principle in effective practice will see them save a lot of time and attain optimum success.

80/20 is counter intuitive. Students who get rid of their threats to optimum productivity actually start experiencing more success and become more productive. Utilizing this principle requires dedication and resolve along with thought.

Focus your energy on the right aspects of your education because 80% of all the effects arise from 20% of the causes. Understand that 20% of your tests and assignments account for 80% of your grade. With this reality, students need to get the information on what the assignments are and what weight they have towards the final grade.

Once equipped with the information on the tests and assignments and their weights, the focus now should be on those assignments and tests with the highest weight that will add up to almost 80% of the final grade. Most of the students' energy should be pressed on such assignments. Get to know the specific aspects to be tested to avoid using a lot of time to study what is not necessary.

Studying is a key to academic success. It has been established that one gets 80% of the studying in just 20% the actual time spent on studying. DO YOU BELIEVE THIS? Let's see the reality of the statement: amidst studying you will be distracted severally, you find yourself re-reading, fantasizing about the future, thinking of other things or going to take a cup of tea. If there are 5 hours available for studying, 20% is one hour. This means that you will need one hour of studying to achieve the target of 5 hours of studying.

For example, in preparation for exams the Pareto principle will always apply in most cases. It goes without say that 80% of the exam results are contributed by just 20% of the effort applied. When preparing for an exam, you will have different materials to read including the notes written, textbooks, lab materials in the case of any and some supplementary reading. But in reality, only a fraction of everything to be studied has worth in the final mark. Take a case study of algebra. Most of the class time is spent on deriving a number of formulas. When it comes to the final exams, it surprises many to find that none of the derivations are needed in the final exam. On the flipside, give more attention to the amount that gives in most yield. Do not subdue the brains to study everything equally.

CONCLUSION

Succeeding or increasing one's productivity in school isn't that hard. With self-discipline and a desire to learn, success will come to you naturally. If you sit back and relax, you will have troubles to get by.

There will be hindrances on the way that may prevent students to attain optimum productivity. There may be encounters regurgitating lecture material, over-generalization during exams, bits of carelessness and other distractors.

If you want to graduate from a school, you would have to make it a point to get a passing grade. Better yet, you should take the effort to excel, not just pass. Excelling needs the right techniques, good habits, adequate preparation and positive emotions. When you excel, you'll be putting a feather on your cap when you finally pursue the career that follows after your graduation. The same goes true for aviation: excelling in ground school would be a very good mark on your curriculum vitae.

Now, don't be intimidated. Just like any other type of school, it is highly possible to excel in your school. It's not just for the elites! In fact, they only become the elite because they tried hard to become the elite. You, too, have what it takes to be at the top of your class in flight school and graduate not only with a passing grade, but with bright colors!

So, you see, it's not that difficult to excel in school. All it really takes is the positive attitude and the willingness to learn more in order to be one of the top students in the class.

Thank you again for downloading this book on *"Productivity Secrets For Students: The Ultimate Guide To Improve Your Mental Concentration, Kill Procrastination, Boost Memory And Maximize Productivity In Study"* and reading all the way to the end. I'm extremely grateful.

If you know of anyone else who may benefit from the informative tips presented in this book, please help me inform them of this book. I would greatly appreciate it.

Finally, if you enjoyed this book and feel that it has added value to your life in any way, please take a couple of minutes to share your thoughts and post a REVIEW on Amazon. Your feedback will help me to continue to write the kind of Kindle books that helps you get results. Furthermore, if you write a simple REVIEW with positive words for this book on Amazon, you can help hundreds or perhaps thousands of other readers who may want to enhance their life have a chance getting what they need. Like you, they worked hard for every penny they spend on books. With the information and recommendation you provide, they would be more likely to take action right away. We really look forward to reading your review.

Thanks again for your support and good luck!

If you enjoy my book, please write a POSITIVE REVIEW on amazon.

-- Lucy Love --

CHECK OUT OTHER BOOKS

Go here to check out other related books that might interest you:

Marriage Heat: 7 Secrets Every Married Couple Should Know On How To Fix Intimacy Problems, Spice Up Marriage & Be Happy Forever

https://www.amazon.com/dp/B01ITSW8YU

Smart Kids Smart Money: The Ultimate Parent's Guide To Teaching Kids About Earning, Saving, Giving, Spending And Investing Money Wisely

https://www.amazon.com/dp/B01KEZVFU4

Legal Vocabulary In Use: Master 600+ Essential Legal Terms And Phrases Explained In 10 Minutes A Day

http://www.amazon.com/dp/B01L0FKXPU

English Collocations In Use: Master 500+ Collocations Explained In 10 Minutes A Day

http://www.amazon.com/dp/B01JHUNYZQ

Shortcut To Ielts Writing: The Ultimate Guide To Immediately Increase Your Ielts Writing Scores

http://www.amazon.com/dp/B01JV7EQGG

The Shocking Truth About Sexual Blackmail: The Secrets Cyber Scammers Don't Want You To Know - The World's Best Advice On How To Deal With Sexual Blackmailers

http://www.amazon.com/dp/B01IO1615Y

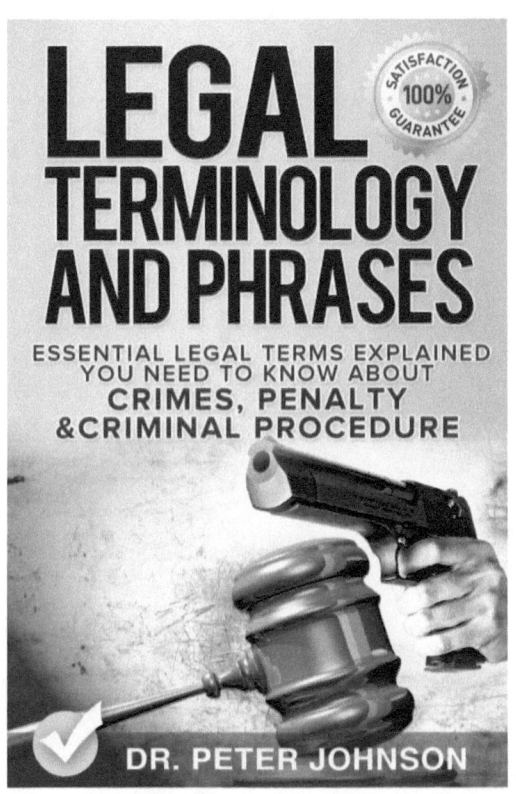

Legal Terminology And Phrases: Essential Legal Terms Explained You Need To Know About Crimes, Penalty And Criminal Procedure

http://www.amazon.com/dp/B01L5EB54Y

Legal Terminology And Phrases: Essential Legal Terms Explained You Need To Know About Civil Law And Civil Procedure

https://www.amazon.com/dp/B01LDLRU0C

Daughter of Strife: 7 Techniques On How To Win Back Your Stubborn Teenage Daughter

https://www.amazon.com/dp/B01HS5E3V6

Parenting Teens With Love And Logic: A Survival Guide To Overcoming The Barriers Of Adolescence About Dating, Sex And Substance Abuse

https://www.amazon.com/dp/B01JQUTNPM

Female Organism: The Best Oral Sex Ever To Give Her A Mind-Blowing Pleasure

https://www.amazon.com/dp/B01KIOVC18